Who Pooped in the Zoo?

Exploring the Weirdest, WACKIEST, GROSSEST & Most surprising Facts About Zoo Poo

by Caroline Patterson

Illustrations by Robb Rath

FARCOUNTRY
PRESS

Credits

Sources:

Davies, Nicola. *Poop: A Natural History of the Unmentionable*. Cambridge, Massachusetts: Candlewick Press. 2004.

Landstrom, Lee Ann and Karen I. Shragg. *Nature's Yucky!* Missoula, Montana: Mountain Press. 2003.

Lewin, Ralph A. *Merde*. New York: Random House. 1999.

Lynch, Wade. *The Scoop on Poop*. Calgary, Alberta: Fifth House Publishing. 2001.

Photo and illustration credits:

All illustrations by Robert Rath.

All photographs, except as noted, © Zoological Society of San Diego, 2007.

The following photographs are courtesy of photos.com: Borders throughout, lion (pg. 11), badger and hyena (pg. 15), grizzly sow and cub (pg. 17), arctic fox (pg. 18), pack rat and mouse (pg. 20), white-tailed deer (pg. 23), robin with nest (pg. 24), black bear cub (pg. 28), cedar waxwing with chicks (pg. 29), gannet, (pg. 31), termite mounds (pg. 32).

Bridgeman Art Library, pg. 25, scarab pectoral, from the tomb of Tutankamun, in the Valley of the Kings at Thebes, c. 1861-52 b.c., New Kingdom (gold, lapis-lazuli, amber et al) by Egyptian, 18th Dynasty (c. 1567-1320 b.c.) ©Egyptian National Museum, Cairo, Egypt / Giraudon/The Bridgeman Art Library Nationality/copyright status: Egyptian/out of copyright.

Image Library of the Royal Saskatchewan Museum, pg. 16, coprolite photo, T. rex coprolite 3.

Nebraska State Historical Society Photographic Collection, pg. 35, emigrant children photo, RG 3314.

Strickland Entomological Museum, used by permission of Gary Anweiler, pg. 33, bird-dropping moth photo.

Talkeetna Historical Society, Talkeetna, Alaska, pg. 36, moose-poop game.

ISBN 10: 1-56037-504-3
ISBN 13: 978-1-56037-504-3

For more information on our books, write Farcountry Press, P.O. Box 5630, Helena, MT 59604; call (800) 821-3874; or visit www.farcountrypress.com.

Library of Congress Cataloging-in-Publication Data

Patterson, Caroline, 1956-
  Who pooped in the zoo? / by Caroline Patterson.
    p. cm.
  Includes index.
  ISBN 978-1-56037-504-3
  1. Animal droppings--Juvenile literature. I. Title.
  QL768.P38 2011
  590--dc22

                        2010005809

Created, produced, and designed in the United States.
Manufactured by
    Paramount Printing Co., Ltd.
    3 Chun Kwong Street
    Tseung Kwan O Ind. Estate
    Hong Kong
    May 2011
    Printed in Hong Kong.

16 15   14 13 12 11   1 2 3 4 5

Table of Contents

The Purpose of Poop

Body Waste: In So Many Words

Poop. Feces. Scat. Guano. No matter what word you use for it, poop is poop. Dark, smelly, squishy, it is the body's way of eliminating waste, whether you are a ten-year-old girl, a lion, or one of the other animals in the zoo. No matter what an animal eats—whether it is gazelles and wildebeests, or mosquitoes and moths—the meal's journey through the body begins when the jaws start chewing. Then the stomach goes into action, producing enzymes that break down the food into a mush. That is the fuel that keeps the body going.

What isn't used as fuel, however, heads off to the intestines, where it meets up with other body trash—such as worn-out blood cells and excess water. They head on down to the colon where, like planes on a runway, they wait their turns to come out of the body as poop.

Elephant poop

Shooting Poop

Some hawks shoot out their poop as far as they can in an effort to keep their wings clean. Most birds, in fact, poop before they take off—they don't want the extra baggage when they are in the air.

P.U.

Some of the smelliest poop belongs to the spiny echidna (also known as the spiny anteater). Yeow! Do they make spiny echidna poop air freshener?

Rabbit to Whale Poop: Differences in Size

For humans, the size of poop is approximately 1 ounce for every 12 pounds of body weight. That means the average doo-doo of an 80-pound boy is approximately 6 ounces. His 150-pound mom's poop weighs 12.5 ounces. Compare that to a blue whale, whose droppings are nearly 1 yard wide and several yards long—about the size of a toboggan. Imagine having to scoop that poop! Rabbit droppings, on the other hand, are the size of small marbles.

Female and male lion

A Wild Ride Through the Body

Whether food is gnashed, pecked, gulped, or delicately speared with a fork, it travels inside an animal's body through the **intestines,** where it mixes with the body's enzymes. The enzymes break the food down into energy for the body before the waste exits out the you-know-what. But what a long trip it takes! Meat-eaters—including humans, lions, and tigers—have intestines 4 to 6 times as long as they are! But plant-eaters take the cake—or the carrot. Bighorn sheep, for example, have intestines nearly 25 times the length of their bodies! Some wild animals have intestines that are even longer. Elephant seals have intestines that are a whopping 720 feet long!

Meat-eater

Plant-eater

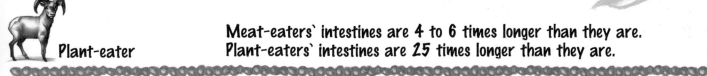

Meat-eaters' intestines are **4 to 6** times longer than they are.
Plant-eaters' intestines are **25** times longer than they are.

Eating

Pooping

Jellyfish

Where's the Exit?

We all know that most animals have a separate exit for their body's waste. But not all animals. Some animals, such as sea anemones and jellyfish, have only one opening in their bodies for eating and pooping. Birds, reptiles, and amphibians all have one opening for eating, and one for peeing and pooping. Mammals, however, have three separate openings: one for eating, one for peeing, and one for pooping.

Brown or Pink, Hard or Soft

Most animals have poop that is brown or black, but the color does vary somewhat according to what the animals eat.

Ever heard of pink poop? It exists! The white or grayish poop of penguins turns pink, believe it or not, when the penguins feast on a small shrimp-like crustacean called krill. Birds that eat red berries in autumn often have poop that is—you guessed it—reddish instead of white. Flamingos eat shrimp and—bingo!—pink poop. Panda poop, on the other hand, is yellow.

Penguin eating krill

What you eat affects the colors in your own bathroom—red meat makes your poop darker, blackberries make it green, beets turn it red, and all that milk that you drink adds a lovely hue of green.

Hard or soft, squishy or brick-like, the **texture** of poop varies. **Carnivores** (animals that eat meat) have long, bumpy **scat** that contains leftovers: old blood cells, bones, fur, and feathers their bodies cannot digest. Carnivores also poop less often than plant-eaters—about once or twice a day. Coyotes, for example, feed on mice and deposit a long, tapered scat once a day that contains fur and mouse bones.

Bats turn themselves into little corkscrews—twisting and turning—in order to keep from pooping on themselves. And, at night, many of the 950 species of bats sleep upside down. In the middle of the night, they wake up, flip right side up, poop, then hang upside down and go back to zzzzz-land. Fruit bats have a "pooping order"; only the top fruit bats get to sleep on the top branches—imagine how unhappy the lowly fruit bat is on the branches below!

Fruit bat

Herbivores (animals that eat plants) eat—and also poop—much more often than carnivores because they have to eat larger quantities of food to get nourished. Your basic barn-yard goose poops nearly five times an hour! Pandas have crumbly poops that contain pieces of bamboo stalks. If giant panda bears eat more bamboo leaves than stalks, their poop is green.

Bird eating red berries

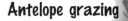

Antelope grazing

Comfort Food

Water content also affects poop. Animals that don't drink a lot of water have very dry scat or poop. Camels, for instance, have droppings so dry you could light them on fire. In order to survive in the desert, camel bodies cannot waste water; their bodies retain all the water that the camels drink, and it does not pass through as waste water. Animals that have plenty of access to water, such as bears, have moister poops.

Camel and calf

Hold Your Nose!

Poop smells because of **bacteria**—and not all poop smells are created equal. This bacteria goes on to produce smelly compounds rich in sulfur (which smells like rotten eggs) and the nitrogen-rich compounds that give farts their smell.

In the wild, orangutans have the smelliest poops because of the durian fruit that they eat. Rabbits, on the other hand, have almost odorless poops. And animal poops smell differently during different times of the year; deer poop smells differently during the mating season than it does during the rest of the year. The smell also is affected by the age and health of the animal.

Animals can tell a great deal about other animals from the smell of their poop. Stallions, for example, can figure out who the number-one male horse is by the smell of his poop. Same with wild rabbits. Black-footed

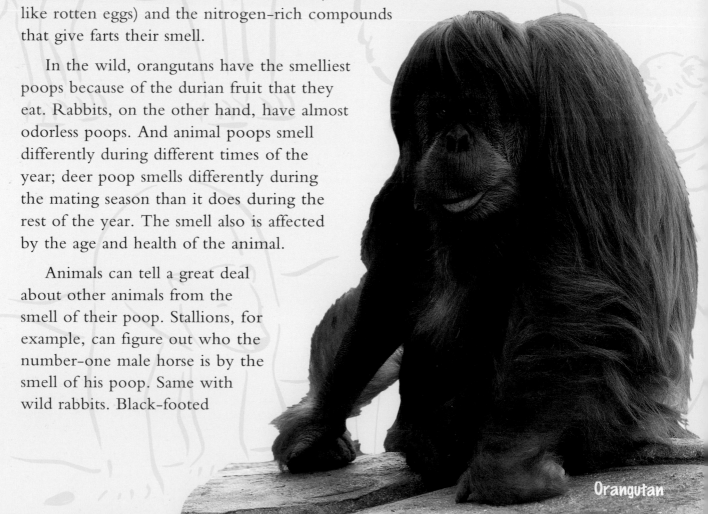
Orangutan

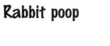
Rabbit poop

Elephant poop

salamander females are said to pick out their mates based on the smell and texture of their poop. The poop tells them: **1** if the guy can catch some good vittles, **2** if he is strong and fit, and **3** if the dude will make a good daddy for the kids. There's one way of finding a mate!

Koala poop

Lion poop

Panda poop

Bird poop

More Than Waste Management

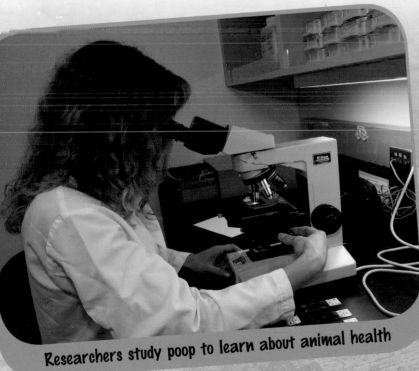
Researchers study poop to learn about animal health

Round and soft, prickly and long, sloppy or pellet-like—poop tells an important story about animals' bodies. Animals, ranging from termites to koalas, use poop to make houses, feed their young, find good mates, and mark their territory. Poop also tells us a lot about the many ways that animals navigate around their worlds using their eyes and noses.

If it's brown, don't put it down: there's a lot to understand about the function of poop. People who study animals spend a good deal of time examining the animal poop. Poop tells them not only what the animals eat, but also about the health of the animal itself and its genetic make-up, for each poop contains some of the animal's DNA.

Hey, That's MINE!

NO TRESPASSING

You may have put a sign on your bedroom door that says: "Keep Out!" Or, on the door of your playroom that says: "This room is for kids only!" Well, animals send similar messages with—you got it!—their poop. By pooping on prey that they kill, by pooping in the middle of game trails that they travel on, and by pooping around the territory that they live in, animals send messages to other animals that say things like: "Hey, this is mine, get your paws off it!" Or "Hey, I'm around, what's up?"

Sumatran tiger

The Invisible (but Stinky!) Fence

A male tiger will mark off his territory—much like your male cat does—by leaving his droppings along the trails in special piles of earth called **scrapes.** This is his (smelly!) way of telling the other animals, "Hey, this is my turf!" A number of animals—including badgers, civets, foxes, muskrats, and otters—also mark their home turf with turds. Spotted hyenas will poop as a group around their territory as a way of marking it.

Muskrat

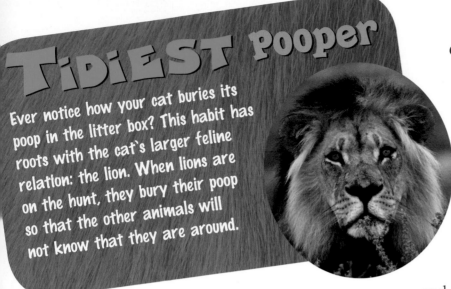

TiDiEST pooper

Ever notice how your cat buries its poop in the litter box? This habit has roots with the cat's larger feline relation: the lion. When lions are on the hunt, they bury their poop so that the other animals will not know that they are around.

Other animals use piles of dung as a way of marking their territory. Sloths, for example, climb down from their trees about once a week to poop in big smelly piles, or **middens,** at the bases of their trees, and some say that they also use these dung piles to woo mates. Speaking for the human species, I'd prefer chocolate and flowers!

Poop Stompin'

Rhinos can amass poop piles nearly 16 feet wide—as wide as four ten-year-old kids lying head-to-toe! And, before it makes a new deposit, the male rhino will use his horn to spread out the older poop. He will also stomp his feet and get them nice and smelly so that the other rhinos will know he's nearby and that he is big, mean, and tough.

African antelopes, too, use dung piles to mark territory. The male antelope will **defecate** (a big word for pooping) on a dung heap as a way of saying to the other males, "Hey man, I'm boss." Among male African antelope, the larger the male, the more often he will poop. And—sort of how we use fences—male antelopes use poop to define the borders of their territory.

Zambian sable antelope

That's My Baby!

Blue-footed boobies do not recognize their own chicks. Instead, the adult blue-footed boobies define their chicks as those inside the rings of their poop. Blue-footed boobies build their nests on the ground where, after time, they become surrounded by rings of white bird poop. When the chicks are hatched, the adult birds know only to feed the chicks inside the poop ring. If some unsuspecting chick wanders outside the ring of poop, the adult bird may not allow it back in the nest—and may even attack it!

Blue-footed booby

The Bulletin Board

Some animals, such as wolves, spend so much of their time alone that they leave their poop along the trail as a way of telling the rest of the gang where they are—just as we might leave a note on the counter that says, "Gone shopping. Be back at 5:00."

Wolves from North America poop along their hunting trails as a way of letting the other wolves in the pack know where and who they are.

Peccaries that live in the South American jungle also use poop as a way to keep in touch with one another—kind of like a message board. The pigs spend their days out in the jungle, hunting for food, so the only way they have of keeping in touch is through their big old poop pile in the middle of their turf. The peccaries

Chacoan peccaries

come back to the poop pile to check in, and a sniff of fresh poop tells them volumes: what the others are eating, which peccary is looking for a mate, which peccary is pregnant, and which one is top pig.

Who's Calling?

Rabbits, too, use poop as a kind of message board. They all poop on the same mound of poop. Pretty soon, the pile of poop is a great big message board, telling them which rabbits are around, which rabbits are pregnant, and which rabbits are eating well.

The catlike genets, from southern Europe, are very solitary animals that use poop as a way of keeping up with the others. They find a high rock or a big tree, poop on it, and then the other genets passing through the area go to this latrine to figure out who is around, who is a rival, and who is a friend.

Next time you are hiking and you come across wild animal scat on the trail, you may wonder if it is a no trespassing sign, a message, or a calling card!

Large spotted genet

MESSIEST Pooper

Hands down, the messiest pooper is the male hippo. He sprays his poop. As his bottom moves from side to side, his poop flies in all directions—a lovely bathroom habit called "muck spreading." This is the male hippo's way of showing the other animals that he is one of the biggest dudes on the block. In addition, hippo males and females twirl their tails, propeller-style, which helps them spread the poop.

Group Poop

Animal Bathrooms

If you're at a football game and you need to use the bathroom, what do you do? You head for the men's or women's restroom, that group of stalls where we humans do our business. We humans, however, weren't the first to think of that! Animals, too, poop in group areas that are known as *latrines*.

Guanacos, relatives of llamas, pick out special pooping areas, or latrines, that are away from their grazing areas. The guanacos even take turns pooping—just as we humans wait in those long restroom lines during half-time. Males from other species, such as blackbacks and African dik-diks, also use latrines.

Guanacos

The Meaning of Poop

The word "poop" comes from the Middle English word *poupen* or *popen*, to blow a horn, toot, or fart. The word poop for **feces** came into use around 1900.

Defining Turf

These animal latrines, however, are used for a lot more than just a quick bathroom break. Take the naked mole-rat, for example, from eastern Africa. The naked mole-rats live entirely underground in elaborate mazes and in colonies of up to 300 members. In their colonies, they have special areas picked out for pooping. One might think this is to keep the burrows clean, but the mole-rats like to go in and roll around in all that poop. The poop's smell is a way for mole-rats to distinguish between friends and enemies!

Naked mole-rat

LEAST APPETIZING Use of Poop

Wolverines and hyenas, when they are done feeding on a dead animal, poop all over the remains to save it for later. It is their way to telling other animals to bug off. It's theirs!

Hyena

Down in South America, giant otters create large family latrines alongside riverbanks as a way of sending other otters a loud, stinky message: "Hey, there's a whole bunch of us, so don't even think of hanging out here."

Badgers also live in family groups and use latrines to tell other animals, "Hey, this is my place!" Above ground, badgers scratch out a shallow spot for a latrine, while underground in their burrows, they designate special chambers for their potties. Badgers use two types of latrines: larger ones for the territory-marking poops; smaller ones for everyday poops.

Badger

Australian wombats leave their droppings in piles to mark their home turf. And, because generations upon generations of wombats have lived together in the same old caves, the poop is piled up very high!

Australian wombat

That's One Old Poop!

How about 70 million years old? Fossilized dinosaur poop, known as **COPROLITES**, can tell us many things about the behavior of the extinct animals. Coprolites tell us not only who was dinner, but how that dinner was had.

A TYRANNOSAURUS REX coprolite, for example, that contains a triceratop's bone fragments with T. rex teeth marks tells us that the T. rex ate the triceratops by tearing it apart with its teeth.

Coprolite

Messages in a Turd

For animals, poop is like an encyclopedia—it can tell animals a lot about the world around them. An animal's poop helps identify it, just like a fingerprint or paw print. Poop can identify an animal's sex or gender because a female's poop smells different than a male's poop. And, because a young animal's poop smells different than an older animal's, dung can be a signpost to predators who like tender young fawns or elk calves: "Hey, delicious, tender vittles this way!"

Predators judge the freshness of scat to see how close by the animals are; they will ignore old dried-up droppings on the trail, but when they come upon fresh droppings, they will stop, look, and listen. Especially when it comes from an animal that they like to eat.

Predators: Vamoose!

On the other hand, if you are a rabbit and you come across fresh wolf scat, that's a sign that you want to head the other direction—and quick! Animals stay away from the poop of animals that eat them. Voles avoid fox poop. Cows and sheep avoid any food that contains a whiff of coyote or mountain lion droppings.

Sometimes, too, animals will poop on top of other animals' poop, though it is not known if this is a calling card or a threat. Bears, for example, will sometimes poop on cow patties—and dogs on anthills.

Climbing Down to Poop

Sloths live high in the trees, eating leaves. Every four days or so—whether it needs to or not—it climbs down to poop in its own private latrine at the base of the tree. How does it check to see what the other sloths are doing? It goes to sniff the huge, smelly dung piles at the bases of their trees.

Sloth

Grizzly sow and cub

WHAT'S for Lunch?

Eating Poop

Some animals dine on dung. We are disgusted when we see our dogs or cats do this, but among some wild animals this is a common occurrence known as **coprophagia.** It sounds disgusting, but it serves a purpose—without it we'd all be buried, chin-deep, in poop.

Some animals, such as lions, chase down and kill their prey and dine on the fresh meat; others like their meals pre-digested.

Striped hyena from India

Scavengers, such as jackals and spotted hyenas, follow the lion to dine not only on the leftover scraps, but also on the lion poop itself! This way, they, too, can benefit from that fresh meat, with a whole lot less effort.

A Pre-digested Meal

In the Arctic, the ivory gull and the arctic fox follow the polar bear to get the scraps of seal meat that are left over in the polar bear poop. In North America, turkey vultures—often seen by roadsides eating animals that have been hit by cars—also occasionally eat coyotes' meaty poops.

Arctic fox

Turkey vulture eating poop

GROSS-OUT
poop stories

And I mean gross! A snowy sheathbill bird will eat tapeworms from the poop of a chinstrap penguin, even if the tapeworm is still attached to the penguin's bottom!

And, if turkey vultures are attacked, their primary means of defense is not their claws or their teeth—it is their vomit! Turkey vultures will projectile-vomit on predators in order to defend themselves.

The most extreme poop picknicker is the snowy sheathbill in Antarctica, which will eat just about anything, no matter if it is dead, stinky, or disgusting. The sheathbill is also known to frequently eat the droppings of the penguins that it wanders among—sometimes fresh from their bottoms!

Snowy sheathbill eating penguin poop

Natural Recycling

Other animals eat poop for its nutritional value, though personally I'd rather eat my spinach! Many small rodents, such as squirrels, rabbits, mice, and rats, do not have the long intestines of, say, bighorn sheep, so they have to send their food through their bodies twice in order to get all the nutrients from the grass they eat. And that means eating their poop. The first and second sets of poops even look different. The first is soft

Shortest
Time between Poops

Rabbits have been known to poop as much as 500 pellets a day—that's 20 poops an hour! It's a wonder they have time to do anything else.

Eastern cottontail

and black and full of partly digested grasses; the second is much drier. Now that's recycling!

If caged rats are not allowed to eat their own **feces,** sometimes they develop vitamin deficiencies—just as you would if you didn't eat vegetables. In some cases, turds may make up nearly one-quarter of a rodent's diet. Some animals eat their poop twice because it runs through their systems so quickly.

Check this out: For humans, it takes approximately 16 hours to go from food to feces. For elephants, digestion takes from 23 to 26 hours. For some small animals, such as shrews, it takes 1 hour. This means that not much is digested along the way, so they snack on their poop again just to make the most of their meal.

Pack rat

Mouse

Give Me Your Young & Your Thirsty

Longest
Time without Pooping

Grizzly bears in the wild den up in the winter. And when they den up—guess what?—they don't poop. During their long winter's nap, an internal plug forms in their bodies that keeps them from pooping. That first spring bowel movement can be as big as a baseball bat!

Grizzly bear

Many other leaf-eating animals eat poop, which some say is similar to chewing the cud. Colts sometimes snack on their mother's droppings. Lizards, such as the desert iguana, may eat their own dung for the moisture when the weather is hot and dry, just as elephants may do in a time of drought.

Desert iguana

AW, MOM!

Some Snack!

You may whine when your parents make you eat vegetables and drink milk to stay healthy. Well, don't complain! Some baby animals have to eat their mother's poop in order to be healthy. And, in order to keep their babies hidden, some female animals eat their babies' poop so that predators do not smell the tasty, defenseless animals and decide to make a meal of them.

Koala

Eating Mum's Poop

Now let's face it. To us, a baby eating its mother's poop sounds downright disgusting. But, among animals, it serves a very important function. Take the koala, for example. Koalas live on eucalyptus leaves, which are very difficult to digest. Bacteria in the mother's intestine helps her break down the tough eucalyptus leaves— but what about the koala joey?

BRINGING UP BABY

Female mountain lions have to lick the bottoms of the newly born cubs in order to get them to poop or pee. The females then eat and drink the cubs' waste so that the smell does not attract predators. White-tailed and mule deer do this also.

Mountain lion and cub

Poop to Garden Dirt

At the Wig L. Worm's Composting Garden in the Children's Zoo of the **San Diego Zoo**, children can learn how easily mounds of zoo poop can be turned into rich garden dirt with the help of wriggling earthworms.

When the koala joey is ready to stop nursing and start eating, it needs this bacteria to handle its diet of eucalyptus leaves. The only way it can get it is—you guessed it!—by eating its mother's poop. But it isn't ordinary poop. The mother defecates a special, runny kind of poop called "pap" that is rich in the bacteria the baby needs. The joey eats this simple dinner of dung and—presto!—the joey's stomach then contains the bacteria it needs to digest the eucalyptus leaves.

The Generation Gulp

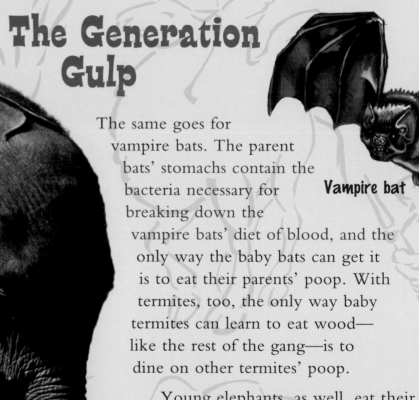

Vampire bat

The same goes for vampire bats. The parent bats' stomachs contain the bacteria necessary for breaking down the vampire bats' diet of blood, and the only way the baby bats can get it is to eat their parents' poop. With termites, too, the only way baby termites can learn to eat wood—like the rest of the gang—is to dine on other termites' poop.

Young elephants, as well, eat their mothers' poop to obtain the bacteria they need to digest the vegetation that they find on the savannah. When they are born, their intestines do not contain these bacteria. Without these necessary bacteria, the elephants

Baby elephant

Giant panda and cub

cannot get all the nutrition from plants. In some cases, they may have to eat poop or die!

Often, microbes have been handed down from generation to generation, just like your great-grandfather's old pocket watch!

Keeping Up with Baby

And then there are the animal mothers that eat baby poop—nature's diaper service, minus the diapers. Many animal females do this not because they love the taste of the dung. They do it to keep their young safe from predators who are always lurking around, looking for a tasty meal.

Housecleaning and Poop

Mothers also eat the waste of their young for housekeeping purposes. Giant pandas, in the wild, house their babies in dens they make in hollowed-out trees that they line with branches, bark, and leaves. The female doesn't go to the bathroom inside the den, and keeps it clean by eating the cub's poop and pee as well.

White-tailed doe and fawn

Robin with chicks in nest

Nest-cleaning

Many songbirds, including robins, clean their nests by taking the tiny sacs of robin poop in their beaks (like we would use our hands) and depositing them far away from the nest. Otherwise baby robins would literally poop themselves out of house and home because the baby birds eat and poop three or four times a day. As the birds become teenagers, they start to do this for themselves. Baby hornbills and kingfishers literally aim their poop so it shoots out of the tree cavities that contain their nests.

Picking Up the Pouch

Kangaroos eat their joeys' scat in order to clean out their pouches. Koalas do this as well—although the pouches are much more difficult to clean and, occasionally, a koala joey smothers in its own you-know-what.

Okapi and calf

Okapis, relatives of giraffes that live in the Congo region of Africa, keep their nests clean because the calves do not poop for a few weeks. The okapis hide their newborn calves in one spot. The calves do not poop until they are between four and eight weeks of age, which keeps predators from sniffing out the newborns.

Kangaroo and joey

King of the Poop-Eaters

Dung, Here We Come

When it comes to eating poop, dung beetles are the undisputed champions! And, face it, life without dung beetles is, well, buried in poop.

Dung beetle

Outback Stories

When buffalo flies killed off many cattle dung beetles in northern Australia, the cattle dung began piling up. The farmers imported twenty species of African dung beetles—and took special care of them, carrying cow dung to the hungry beetles in wagons they called "Meals on Wheels." The dung beetles made the cow patties vanish in two days, instead of lasting up to four years in the dry climate!

Rolling Along

Egyptians thought dung beetles, also called scarab beetles, were sacred. They believed they represented their sun god, Ra, who rolled the sun across the sky and buried it each night. The scarab beetles were carved in precious stones and worn as jewelry.

Egyptian scarab

A Dung Disappearing Act

There are dung beetles for many, many kinds of dung, large or small, wet or dry, round or long and tube-like. There are 7,000 kinds of dung beetles in the world! In Africa, 16,000 beetles can descend upon a pile of elephant poop and make it disappear within several hours. There are dung beetles that feast on cow patties. And there are dung beetles that climb high in the rain forest to scrape monkey poop off the leaves, carry it down to the forest floor, and bury it to soften it. Think of a kind of poop and in many cases there is a beetle that features it as a favorite food.

People are even talking about developing special dung beetles to take care of the dog poop problem in big cities. Now that's a small pooper scooper!

Allen's swamp monkey

Dung beetle

Vernay's ratel baby

Rock and Roll Dung Beetles

Though the dung beetles share a taste for poop, they go about their dining in very different ways. Dung beetles are divided into three types: rollers, tunnellers, and dwellers.

Rollers roll their sheep or rabbit dung into balls that they move into their burrows to eat later on. These balls can weigh as much as fifty times more than the beetle itself!

Tunnellers dig big tunnels under the ground. While males bring them fresh poop, female dung beetles store dung balls in the ends of the tunnels and then lay eggs in the dung piles. When the baby beetles are born, they have a ready supply of fresh poop to eat.

Burrowers find dung and live in it. They make a hole in juicy poop and that's where they live, eating and sleeping, literally eating themselves out of a house. Sometimes other animals, such as African ratels or honey badgers, dig up the balls to feast on the tasty grubs.

Little Johnny Appleseeds

Planting with Poop

Some people say that one man's garbage is another's treasure—and the same might be said of poop. Contained in the waste products of many mammals and birds are not only food, but also the beginnings of new life. The fruit and berries that many animals eat survive the chewing and the digestion and come out in the animals' poop. Berries that are eaten by black bears and pooped out, for example, actually grow better than if the berry seeds were just planted!

Remember those rain forest dung beetles? Well, they bring the monkey poop down from the trees and bury it in the forest floor. This monkey poop contains seeds from the fruit that the monkeys eat. The dung beetle buries those and—bingo!—a new tree is born!

Mistletoe

Birds and Berries

This happens with birds as well. Birds are attracted to bushes with bright berries. They eat up the berries, then fly around, pooping out those berry seeds, planting new huckleberry, hawthorn, holly, and

Black bear cub

honeysuckle bushes. From the poop of cedar waxwings grow rowan or firethorn bushes.

One of the most clever plants at getting birds to do their bidding is mistletoe. Birds—such as robins, thrushes, and blackbirds—eat the mistletoe berries, but when they poop out the seeds, the seeds stick to their bottoms. The birds have to rub their bottoms on rough tree bark or on cracked branches to get the seeds off their bottoms. Then—voila!—mistletoe seeds are planted in the spots where they will grow best.

You can make a list of almost any bird or animal that eats seed-bearing fruit, and most if not all are responsible for planting more of its food with its poop. When you think of it, it is an amazing plan.

Cedar waxwing and chicks

Nature's Gardeners

Cardon cactus

From the **guano** of oilbirds in Venezuelan caves grow tiny forests of white palms. From the guano of fruit-eating bats in Central America are the beginnings of cardon cactuses. Tapirs in Amazonian jungles plant palm seeds. And in Africa, elephants and impalas plant acacias.

And guess who spreads tomato seeds? You and I do! Hardy tomato seeds survive the trip through our bodies, are flushed down the toilet, and end up in sewage treatment facilities, where—eventually—they sprout. Talk about a crazy ride!

In the wild, poop mixed in with the soil can help things grow. Termites chew up wood and use their poop as a fertilizer. They stick their poop together in masses called combs, and use it to grow mushrooms.

A Research Tool

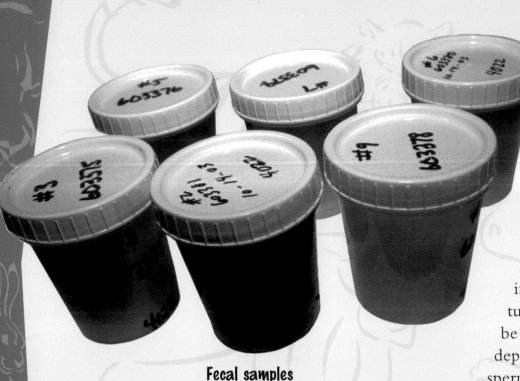

Fecal samples

The leftovers in poop are a wonderful way for scientists to study what animals are eating, especially if they can't watch the creatures eat. A scientist may not be able to dive down to the depths of the ocean where the sperm whale eats, but she can find its leftover meal of squid and sharks in its poop. On the other end of the scale, bats are so small and quick they are hard to see, so examining their leftovers is the best way to figure out what they've been dining on. Under a microscope, researchers can match up insect parts to figure out just how many bugs one animal has eaten.

Scientists collect poop samples to find out all kinds of things, including why an animal changes color at a particular time and why it breeds when it does. By simply scooping up fresh poop, the researcher can study animals—ranging from gorillas to gazelles—without harming or scaring them.

Poop Slang

BAT SPLATS: bat poop
COO PLAB: cow poop in Scotland
DOG DOO: dog poop
ELEPHANT COOKIES: elephant poop
ELK DUDS: elk poop
MOOSE BERRIES: moose poop
SHEEP BUTTONS: sheep poop
ROAD APPLES: horse poop
PELLETS: mouse droppings
RABBIT RAISINS: rabbit poop
COW PATTIES OR COW FLOPS: large cow poops
BUFFALO CHIPS: buffalo poop
WHITEWASH: bird poop

Buildings to Bombs Away

Nature's Glue

Birds don't have cement. They don't have glue. What they have, instead, is poop. Like many animals, birds use it to stick things together. Take African zebra finches, for example. They carefully line their nests with white droppings to make cozy beds for their nestlings.

Secretary bird

Secretary birds often hang out among large mammals to snatch the dried-up animal dung and leaves, which they use to line their nests. Gannets lay their eggs in a scrape (poop and dirt mixed together) and then poop around the eggs to make a rim. Hornbill nestlings are reared in nests made of mud, but if their nests are damaged, the female bird makes the repairs with—you guessed it—her poop. Let's face it, that white sticky guano can come in handy.

Gannet

Abyssinian ground hornbill

31

Termite mounds

Building Homes

When it comes time for millipedes to lay their eggs, they construct a nest out of the building materials close by: their own poop.

Dung High-Rises

Poop Construction

Termites are famous for their poop houses. Tiny ant-sized insects, termites chew up wood, most of which they cannot digest, and it comes right out the other end. Over time, these lumps (or combs) build up into huge **mounds** several feet tall, where huge colonies of termites live.

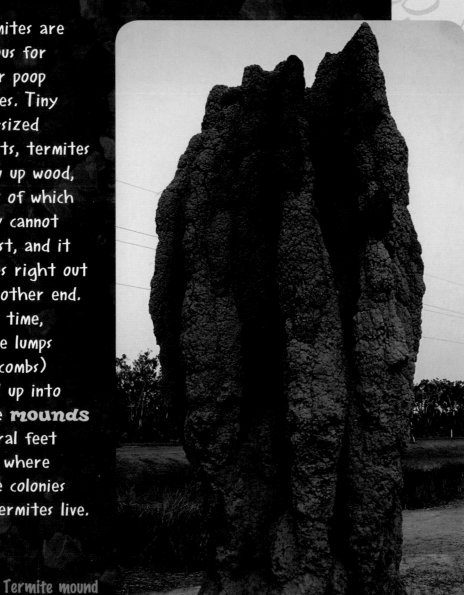
Termite mound

Termites, on the other hand, don't fashion nests from poop. They build houses. These small insects, sometimes known as "white ants," build poop high-rises as tall as houses in places such as African or Australian deserts.

Some animals, though, use poop to fortify or make stronger the home that they have. In the dry forests of Australia, termites eat the soft wood at the center of eucalyptus trees. This hollows out the trees, which then create homes for many other small creatures, including possums and frogs, that drop their poop inside the tree and make it grow stronger.

Disguises and Dispatches

On top of being used as a building material, poop can be used as bait to attract prey, just as you might put a worm on a fishing hook.

The assassin bug loves to eat termites, so in order to conceal itself from its prey, it covers its back with termite droppings.

Other insects use poop as protection. The coloring of bird-dropping moths provides them **camouflage** from being eaten by birds. Their name describes their disguise. Bird-dropping spiders, such as the death's head spider and the orchard spider, use a similar disguise to protect themselves from hungry birds or wasps.

And don't get too close to the grey-and-white jaeger bird in the Arctic. If you venture too close to its nest of chicks, it will fly up in the air and then unload—wham-Cover your head!

Bird-dropping moth

Oddest Cooling System

When storks and vultures get too warm, they aren't able sweat to cool off, as you and I do. Instead, to survive in the hot desert, the birds squirt runny poop down their legs to cool off. As gross as it sounds, the watery poop evaporates and cools the bird's body. The birds shift from one leg to the other, squirting poop down their legs as often as every 2 minutes, until they are more comfortable.

Stork

33

Fertilizer, Fuel, & Earrings?

The Wide World of Poop

Animals aren't the only ones that use poop for building houses or growing crops. Humans have used animal poop for a long, long time for growing plants, heating their houses, cooking food, building homes, making jewelry—and even for playing games.

Manure spreader

Fertilizer

Although people don't use poop as food, farmers around the world spread poop, or **manure,** on their fields to help grow their crops. Whether they are tossing turds from a basket or using large motorized manure spreaders, farmers from China to America use the manure of pigs, cows, llamas, chickens, and even seabirds because it enriches the soil and helps their plants to grow.

A farmer spreading manure in a rice field

Fuel

Poop has been and still is a popular fuel. From ancient times, people in dry climates gathered animal poop to use as fuel for cooking food or heating their homes. From 1841 to the mid-1860s, when the emigrants crossed the Great Plains in the United States, many of their children were assigned the task of gathering dried buffalo chips—or poop—to burn in the campfires at night. In India, cow dung is still used as fuel in many rural homes, and it is sold in marketplaces. In Tibet, yak dung is collected as fuel, prized over sheep or goat dung.

Emigrant children collecting buffalo chips

These days, methane or bio-gas is a valuable alternative source of energy for heating our houses and cooking food. Produced by aged poop, it has been used around the world as a source of heat and electricity. An Englishman even built a car that he claimed ran on methane produced from chicken droppings!

From Huts to Photo Albums

The Masai of East Africa use poop to cover their huts, a bit like we might use stucco. After they build a hut of sticks and grass, the women hut-builders mix fresh cow poop and water and, with their hands, smooth the muck over the sides of the hut. Under the hot African sun, this dries into a tough, protective outer wall.

Masai hut

Around the world, poop is being made into a number of different products. At some zoos you can buy paper, journals, photo albums, and even bookmarks made from panda or elephant poop.

The Masai once fashioned cow dung into a crown for a bride. In the United States, we have moose poop earrings in Maine and Alaska, home of many moose—endless sources of the raw material. The earrings are made of genuine one-inch moose droppings, coated in polyurethane.

Moose-dropping earrings

Children play the moose poop toss at the Talkeetna, Alaska Moose Dropping Festival

Cow Chip Checkers?

American emigrants entertained themselves on the long trip across the Great Plains by seeing who could throw a buffalo chip the farthest. From this tradition emerged the Cow Chip Throwing Festival that has been held in Beaver, Oklahoma, each April since 1970. Winners must throw a cow chip of at least six inches in diameter, selected from the official "dung truck." The festival also chooses a championship cow chip, the "Dried-in-the-Sun-King."

Not to be outdone, Alaska's Talkeetna Historical Society holds a Moose Dropping Festival each year in late June, where shellacked and numbered moose poop is hauled up into the air and then dropped on a bull's-eye. Winners are those whose moose poop falls closest and farthest from the bull's-eye.

A Hot Steaming Cup of WHAT?

Palm civet poop, that's what. It is the source of the most expensive coffee in the world. Called Kopi Luwak, it costs $160 a pound! The palm civet, a cat-sized animal, eats coffee berries, digests the husks, and poops out the coffee beans whole. Their digestive process ferments the beans and gives them a heavenly taste that gourmet coffee drinkers crave. But who was the brave soul that first discovered this?

POOP FOR PEOPLE

Dung is a very useful substance for th Maori, the indigineous people of New Zealand, and this is reflected in their language. Some say that the Maori have 35 different words for dung.

Zoo Poop

Load of elephant poop

What Do You Do with Zoo Poop?

When you have a zoo of thousands of animals, you also have a heck of a lot of poop to get rid of. The 4,000 animals at the San Diego Zoo produce 4 to 5 tons of poop daily—that's half the weight of a school bus! And keepers can't just flush all that down the drain. They have to hose it down, filter it out, or shovel it out each day to keep the animal areas clean.

A Poop Journey

So what happens to all that dung? After collecting the poop, zookeepers take the poop to a central concrete area where it is separated. Carnivore and primate poop—from lions, tigers, and apes—is bagged and sent straight to the dump. Poop from plant-eating animals is mixed with plant clippings, leaves, and straw to make **compost,** or fertilizer.

Ron, an elephant keeper at the San Diego Zoo

Doo at the Zoo

Many zoos sell compost made from the poop of elephants, rhinoceroses, hippos, and zebras as fertilizer for gardens. The compost is good not only because it recycles the poop but because it helps the gardens grow by putting nutrients into the soil. The Toronto Zoo uses zoo poop as compost to fertilize the zoo's 1,500 plants—such as thc banana plants, screw pine plants, and vines in the IndoMalay Pavilion. The Woodland Park Zoo in Seattle sells Zoo Doo. It's so popular that people line up in September and March for the Fecal Fest in order to buy fertilizer made from giraffe, oryx, and gazelle poop.

Poop to Power

What else can we do with zoo poop? Could it be used to power a train? Lights? Toilets for the entire zoo? Is that the stuff of science fiction? A sick joke? Think again. Zoos around the country are exploring plans to turn animal waste into electric power. The Toronto Zoo is working on a **bio-gas** plant that will convert zoo poop and vegetable waste into electricity. Someday the plant will produce enough power to cover one-third of the zoo's electric bill! The power for the Denver Zoo's Asian Tropics exhibit is provided by—you guessed it!—zoo poop mixed with trash that runs through a special system called **biomass gasification.**

Who Scoops the Most Poop?

Definitely the elephant keeper! At most zoos, nearly half of the manure collected is elephant poop. Elephants have large, Tootsie-roll-shaped poops called boluses that weigh between 4 and 6 pounds, and each elephant poops about 100 pounds a day. Koalas produce nearly 200 dark, gummy-bear-sized pellets every day. The Bactrian camel, an endangered species, has about 10 poops a day. The lizard keeper has the best job: a lizard poops just once a day.

Glossary

Bacteria – microscopic organisms that make poop smelly

Bolus – elephant poop

Camouflage – a behavior or disguise an animal uses to hide from predators

Carnivore – animal that eats meat

Coprolite – fossilized dinosaur poop

Coprophagia – the act of an animal eating poop

Defecate – a fancy way of saying poop

DNA – This stands for deoxyribonucleic acid, which is a scientific word used for talking about genes (not the kind that you wear, but the kind that determine your hair and eye color, and whether or not you can roll your tongue).

Feces – scientific, and more polite way, of saying poop

Guano – seabird or bat poop

Herbivore – animal that eats plants

Intestines – the long, windy tubes in an animal's body that carry and absorb digested food

Latrine – special area that animals use for pooping or peeing

Manure – poop when it is used on a field to help plants grow

Middens – special piles of poop left by animals, such as sloths or rhinos, to mark territory

Mounds – tall houses built of termite poop

Scat – wild animal poop

Scrapes – special mounds of poop mixed with dirt left by tigers to mark their territory

Texture – the consistency of something; whether or not it is thick or thin, chunky or smooth

Index